# THE MYSTERY OF THE POWER OF REMEMBRANCE

**PASTOR NANA BEDIAKO**

ISBN:9798333538451

## DEDICATION

This book is dedicated to my lovely wife Linda,
My daughters Jada and Eliana, the CMIA family,
Remembering all those who have been a blessing in my life and ministry.
All my friends and family,
And finally you

# CONTENTS

# FORWARD

I first met Reverend Nana Bediako about ten years ago, and from the beginning, he has exemplified honor and integrity. His kind words and unwavering support have always been accompanied by actions of love and compassion.

Reverend Nana's book, "The Power of Remembrance," is a testament to his life and principles. He embodies the essence of remembering, valuing those whom God places in his path, irrespective of the passage of time.

As I pen this foreword, he remains true to his practice of remembrance. Reverend Nana's commitment to remembrance is evident in his detailed and heartfelt writing. He meticulously guides the reader through his experiences, providing profound insights and lessons. Remembrance, as he illustrates, is pivotal in unlocking life's potential and understanding one's purpose.

This concept is akin to holding the key to one's destiny, which can be lost if not remembered. The importance of remembering is a central theme in this book, demonstrating that even God the Father remembers us. Galatians 3:13-14 reminds us of Jesus's sacrifice, highlighting the significance of being remembered by God.

This book serves as a powerful reminder of God's love and the biblical precedent of remembrance, as seen in how God remembered the children of Israel, aiding them through prophets and blessings. I would like to leave you with several scriptures that reinforce the importance of remembering God's goodness and the people He places in our lives:

- Exodus 3:7-9: God sees and remembers.
- Acts 9:3-4: Paul's remembrance of Jesus.
- Isaiah 43:26: Remembrance for resolution.
- Deuteronomy 8:17-18: Remembering God's empowerment.
- Joshua 1:7-8: Remembering God's words to Moses.

As you read "The Power of Remembrance," may you be inspired to remember the goodness of God and the significant people He has sent into your life.

Apostle Dr. Alexander Gray
Founder of Living Love Ministries International Bronx, NY

# ACKNOWLEDGMENT

I can never forget every single person I have encountered or met on my path to greatness, pursuing my God-given gift and purpose. This book can't have enough pages to record my profound admiration and gratitude. I wish to thank every person the Lord has brought into my life and inspired, touched, and illuminated me through their presence, love, guidance, and pristine advice.

I am profoundly grateful to Apostle Dr. Kwabena Akufo, Lady Peggy Akufo and Apostle Dr. William Shalders, who saw this great potential in me, guided me, and pushed me beyond my limits to write my third book.

Rev. Azigiza, the love is deep, thank you for everything, I mean everything. My brother, friend, bishop and pastor. The best is yet to come.

Thank you, Apostle Alexander Gray, for telling me years ago about this era of my life.

I appreciate Superintendent Daniel Quartey, and Rev. Arthur Bryant & family, Pastor Samuel Ampong, Pastor Edward Amponsah for generously contributing and sharing your wisdom.

One of my favorite African proverbs says that when you see a turtle on a fence, it certainly did not get there on its own. There are many people that I can't even list who have made a tremendous impact on my life. Some have given me encouragement, spiritual guidance, advice, love, and more.

Apostle William and Belinda Shalders, I love you both for your advice, encouragement, teaching, and financial support since I entered the Pastoral Ministry. God bless you richly.

To Rev. Assuo Mensah and Lady Kirby Assuo Mensah, here is all the encouragement and mentorship you gave me through the years. Rev. Mark Asante Manu and Alexander Adu Gyamfi, you have always been there for me through every milestone; thank you. Thank you, Pastor George Aboagye and Pastor Steven Assifuah.

My brother Kingsley Manche and family, Minister Emmanuel Ntim and family whatever you've done behind the scenes; God will always reward you publicly. Minister Alston, I am grateful for your endless support. Elder Ailen, Ufuoma and family, I am forever grateful. God brought you into my life for such a time as this and appreciate you all so much.

To the members and leadership of Change Makers International Assembly Garfield, New Jersey, The Apostolic Church USA, the Men's Movement, the Witness Movement, and all the Apostles, Pastors, Elders, Deacons, and Deaconesses, thank you all.

Team Bediako, thank you for your patience and for giving Dad time to care for the Kingdom businesses.

Finally, my Heavenly Father, without you, I am nobody.

## INTRODUCTION

Have you ever witnessed an event that made you tell yourself, I will never forget this day? Have you ever been in a terrible situation and you said to yourself, I wish I never remembered this day? Are there events you've blotted out of your memory and those that you have typically engraved in your brain?

As humans, forgetting is inevitable; therefore, it's important to intentionally remember the good deeds of people who have positively impacted our lives and all the blessings of the Lord.

Remembrance is an essential aspect of Christianity. As believers, we are encouraged and strengthened by remembering the faith and deeds of those who have gone before us. We recognize the promises of God's word; as we do so, our confidence is built on trusting God and living in his truth.

The theme of remembrance is interwoven throughout the book of Deuteronomy. Moses constantly encourages the Israelites to remember what the Lord did for them in the wilderness and what he required of them as they entered the Promised Land.

We must remember the state in which Jesus found us—lest we forget that we were broken and now are repaired and made like new. God's glory fills the cracks in our lives, and His healing light shines from within our souls. We have been given a new mind, a new speech, and a new attitude—a new life!

Remembrance of God's goodness, breakthrough, favor, and mercy builds up strong trust and faith in the Lord Almighty. Our failure to trust God stems from forgetting the great things God does for us, especially in our past. Forgetfulness can prevent us from moving forward and achieving our dreams and goals due to the fear of the unknown; however, if you can trust God, who has brought you this far, you know He will surely keep you through.

The multiple memorials throughout the journey from

Egypt to the promised land were made so that the people of Israel could teach their children about the great things God has done in the past and the great things that God is about to do in the future. The children seeing these stones will likely create a memorable image in their minds and be passed on to future generations.

Every year or so, I read back through my journals. Each time I reminisce about how God has been so faithful in my life, I am moved by the joy of the Lord, which gives me the strength to keep moving forward. I remember times when I felt lost and afraid, but God was at work in ways I couldn't see at the time.

I traveled to the United States at twenty to begin a new life. I didn't know many people, and I had no parents, but Christ and Christ alone. I had to depend on God solely for everything. So, keeping a journal has helped me and continues to help me, and I hope it will help you, too. God bless you for reading on.

# 1 CHAPTER

# THE SCIENCE OF REMEMBRANCE AND WHY WE FORGET

Have you ever witnessed an event that made you tell yourself, I will never forget this day? Have you ever been in a terrible situation and you said to yourself, I wished I never remembered this day? Are there events you've blotted out of your memory and those that you have typically engraved in your brain? Do you have flashbacks? Some names, places, events, songs, or sounds bring dark or beautiful memories.

In this book, we will explore the power of remembrance. Although there are many weapons in the Kingdom, I consider remembrance one of my favorite and most powerful weapons for winning battles, overcoming obstacles, and surviving storms.

Is forgetting part of life? Surprisingly yes. No wonder God constantly reminded the Israelites not to forget his blessings, protections, deliverance, provisions, and statutes. Research has found that approximately 56% of information is forgotten within an hour, 66% after a day, and 75% after six days.

## WHAT DOES IT MEAN TO FORGET

The definition of forgetting is the loss or change in information that was previously stored in short-term or long-term memory. It can be sudden or gradual, as old memories are lost. While it may usually be expected in many instances, an excessive form or unusual forgetting might indicate a more severe problem.

### DECAY

I believe I am not the only person who has experienced

feeling like a piece of information has just vanished from your memory. Or maybe you know that it's there, but you can't seem to find it. The failure to retrieve a memory is one of the most common causes of forgetting.

Why do these experiences often happen? When one is unable to retrieve information from memory, one possible explanation is known as the decay theory in psychology.

According to this theory, a memory trace is created anytime a new theory is formed. These memory traces will begin to fade and disappear over time, as the Decay theory suggests. It's explained that if the information is retrieved and rehearsed, it will eventually be recovered.

Research shows that a problematic issue with this theory is that memories that have not been rehearsed or remembered are remarkably stable in long-term memory.

Some research also suggests that the brain actively prunes memories that become unused, a process known as active Forgetting. As memories accumulate, those that are not retrieved eventually become lost.

## MOTIVATED FORGETTING

In life, there are certain traumatic or disturbing events or experiences that people may actively work to forget. Painful memories can be hurtful and can stir anxiety, so sometimes, we may want to eliminate them. The two basic forms of motivated forgetting are suppression, which is a conscious form of Forgetting, and repression, which is an unconscious form of forgetting.

There are many coping mechanisms in which forgetting painful memories and trauma may help people who have gone through such experiences.
Painful events might not be entirely ignored, but trying to forget vivid details of traumatic events can help cover difficult emotions that are linked to those dark memories, which makes it easier to deal with those sad experiences.

Many world events can never be forgotten, such as Independence Day, world wars, world sports events like the Olympics, terrorist attacks like 9/11, natural disasters, modern inventions, space explorations, and pandemics like Covid-19 in 2020, as well as world plaques, just to mention a few. We can also talk about politics, like the first black president in the United States.

These events cannot be forgotten and will be passed on from one generation to the other. How many holidays exist? Every holiday is instituted for a nation or a people to remember a person, persons, group, and events. It's a way to help people remember. Look at the monument built at the Twin Towers' site. Generations will come and learn about that event forever, not forgetting events like Pearl Harbor, the Hiroshima bombing, the Holocaust, etc.

Memorial Day celebration, for instance, allows us to reflect on our memory places. These places, I think, house the things we value and the parts of our lives that matter to us. Some valuable people have invested in our lives directly or indirectly. Many pastors have impacted my journey to the office of a pastor. These musicians saw the gift of music in me when I had no clue, those who inspired me and prophesied to me about an era in my life when I would become an author; these people are what I call "people memories." People's memories are people who love, assist, support, fund and are always there to celebrate your growth and success. They can include family, employers, personal friends, and even critics.

There are places in your life that, through the years, have become your personal memory places. Some of these places may be extremely painful and may stir uncomfortable memories. Some of these places may bear secrets known to only you. Some dark memories may include the complicated steps we've taken, wounds we have endured, lessons we have learned, and changes and detours we have made to continue walking in divine directions. Some events in our lives were initially disappointing and painful, but with time, we understood it was all on the agenda of God. It makes one love the scripture, "All things will work together for our good."

Give thanks in all things. We thank God for our memory of places. God instructed Moses to write down many of the places the Israelites settled during their journey via the wilderness to the Promised Land. Memory places are essential to our Christian walk; they help bring us a sense of purpose.

Today, how far we have come, and they prompt us to keep moving to a life destination that has ultimate value to us.

Now, let's look at Numbers 33:1-9 (NIV)

*1 Here are the stages in the journey of the Israelites when they came out of Egypt by divisions under the leadership of Moses and Aaron.*

*2 At the LORD's command Moses recorded the stages in their journey. This is their journey by stages:*

*3 The Israelites set out from Rameses on the fifteenth day of the first month, the day after the Passover. They marched out defiantly in full view of all the Egyptians,*

*4 who were burying all their firstborn, whom the LORD had struck down among them; for the LORD had brought judgment on their gods.*

*5 The Israelites left Rameses and camped at Sukkoth.*

*6 They left Sukkoth and camped at Etham, on the edge of the desert.*

*7 They left Etham, turned back to Pi Hahiroth, to the east of Baal Zephon, and camped near Migdol.*

*8 They left Pi Hahiroth[a] and passed through the sea into the desert, and when they had traveled for three days in the Desert of Etham, they camped at Marah.*

*9 They left Marah and went to Elim, where there were twelve springs and seventy palm trees, and they camped there.*

Life is a journey characterized by movements - detours, roller coasters, red stops, stop signs, and constructions on the way, which can create a delay. No matter the delays, God will go before thee, and make the crooked places straight: I will break in pieces the gates of brass, and cut in sunder the bars of iron" Isaiah□ 45:2□ □□□□□□

In verse 2, God instructed Moses to keep a written record of their journey. There are many reasons why God wanted the Israelites to record the starting point of the journey and all the various stops they made. Keeping a record helps to measure your progress in life and to develop faith and hope.

Taking stock of where you are now enables you to show gratitude for the fact that you have not arrived yet but are not where you used to be.

The Israelites were not in the promised land yet; however, they were not in Ramsey (Egypt). The Israelites saw many signs and wonders in Egypt, including the ten plaques. At one time, there was full darkness in all of Egypt, but there was light in Goshen, where the Israelites lived. The angel of death came, but the firstborn sons of the Israelites were spared.

The remembrance of these signs should give everyone hope in the Lord.
God knew that humanity could forget His goodness easily, so He urged Moses to maintain a record of past events. They came to the Red Sea on their journey to the promised land. For some people, the Red Sea is the end of their trip. Between you and your destiny stands the mighty Red Sea. Everyone will one day face the Red Sea. They show up in marriages, businesses, churches, etc.

The Israelites are facing the massive Red Sea, and the enormous Egyptian army is behind them. Let's examine what the Israelites said to Moses. This shows how a storm can quickly move human beings to change their minds and forget all the prior miracles they witnessed in Egypt.

**Exodus 14:10-14 (NIV)**

*10 As Pharaoh approached, the Israelites looked up, and there were the Egyptians, marching after them. They were terrified and cried out to the LORD.*

*11 They said to Moses, "Was it because there were no graves in Egypt that you brought us to the desert to die? What have you done to us by bringing us out of Egypt?*

*[12] Didn't we say to you in Egypt, 'Leave us alone; let us serve the Egyptians'? It would have been better for us to serve the Egyptians than to die in the desert!"*

*[13] Moses answered the people, "Do not be afraid. Stand firm and you will see the deliverance the LORD will bring you today. The Egyptians you see today you will never see again.*

*[14] The LORD will fight for you; you need only to be still."*

The journey was short, and the Israelites had forgotten all the miracles and promises. These were the people who were in severe bondage, accessible, and on their way to the promised land.

They experience the first storm and forget everything, wishing they were back serving their masters. God will always make a way in the Red Sea if God sends you on a path; he factors the storms on your way. He goes before you and makes every crooked path straight. Never forget his goodness, as you remember every testimony in your life; it will boost your faith and hope.

After the Red Sea experience, they came to Mara three days later and asked what happened again.

**Let's read- Exodus 15:22-25 (NIV)**

*22 Then Moses led Israel from the Red Sea and they went into the Desert of Shur. For three days they traveled in the desert without finding water.*

*23 When they came to Marah, they could not drink its water because it was bitter. (That is why the place is called Marah.[f])*

*24 So the people grumbled against Moses, saying, "What are we to drink?"*

*25 Then Moses cried out to the LORD, and the LORD showed him a piece of wood. He threw it into the water, and the water became fit to drink.*

*There the LORD issued a ruling and instruction for them and put them to the test.*

In verse 24, the people complained against Moses. As you progress, you will become a state of Marah(bitter situation). Marah represents bitter times and challenging places in life, such as the breakup of a relationship, betrayal, loss of a loved one, backstabbing, and loss of a job. They were thirsty, found water, and excited about it, but it wasn't enjoyable. Have you been in a situation where you find a glimpse of light at the end of the tunnel and get there to realize it was not a light?

Have you experienced shattered hope in your life? This is Marah. But God instructed Moses to pick a particular leaf and dip it in water, which became sweet. The Lord will always give you the refreshment you need on your journey; remember his miraculous hands.

## HOW CAN ONE MINIMIZE FORGETTING

It's impossible to forget adverse events entirely. While some are very easy to do, others are inevitable. However, there are some vital information or events that one might need to remember always. Certain practices may improve forgetfulness, such as exercising and repeatedly reviewing information until you can commit it to memory.

Rehearse the information: Sometimes, the best way to commit something to memory and reduce the chances it will be forgotten is to use the old standby: rehearsal. Go over the information repeatedly until you've committed it to memory.

Please write it down: When all else fails, write down important information to refer to it later.

In some cases, the act of writing it down may help you remember it more later.

While forgetting is often viewed negatively, it can help improve memory. Being able to let go of irrelevant memories and only hold on to the critical information helps keep those saved memories more robust, a phenomenon known as adaptive Forgetting.

## 4 WAYS IN WHICH YOU CAN REMEMBER GOD IN YOUR BUSY LIFE

1. Set a daily recurring calendar notification on your smart devices to remind you to appreciate the Lord's goodness.
2. Got a wall plaque with your favorite verse of remembrance and hand it to a place where you can see daily
3. Your phone's home screen should have an inspiring Scripture instead of what you use now.
4. Please write a message of remembrance and put it in your car. There's no reason in our busy lives we can't remember God.

# 2 CHAPTER

## REMEMBRANCE IS INTENTIONAL

Remember, remembrance, or remind are words that are used almost 300 times in the Bible.

The dictionary definitions of remember include "to bring to mind or think of again," "to keep in mind for attention or consideration," and "to retain in the memory." Remembering Christ, then, involves thinking about him often and focusing on his teachings and his atonement for our sins.

As humans, forgetting is inevitable; therefore, it's important to intentionally remember the good deeds of people who have positively impacted our lives and all the blessings of the Lord. We will be looking at some scriptures about the power of remembrance, which, 300 times, means that there is a level of emphasis placed on this act.

***2 Timothy 2:8***

*Remember that Jesus Christ, of the seed of David, was raised from the dead according to my gospel.*

***2 Peter 1:12***

*For this reason, I will not be negligent in reminding you constantly of these things, though you know and are established in the present truth.*

***Luke 22:19***

*And He took bread, gave thanks, broke it, and gave it to them, saying, "This is My body, which is given for you; do this in remembrance of Me."*

God has always instructed His people to remember the things He has done for His people, so the miracles of the past continue to have an effect even in our present day. God is so familiar with humanity and knows how we can forget easily. Therefore, He directs us to use many different forms and memorials to help us always remember His miraculous hand upon us. We will look at some of the unique ways He directs us to stay on the path of remembrance.

***Joshua 4:1-9(NIV)***

*1 When the whole nation had finished crossing the Jordan, the Lord said to Joshua,*
*2 "Choose twelve men from among the people, one from each tribe,*
*3 and tell them to take up twelve stones from the middle of the Jordan, from right where the priests are standing, carry them over with you, and put them down where you stay tonight."*

*4 So Joshua called together the twelve men he had appointed from the Israelites, one from each tribe,*
*5 and said to them, "Go over before the ark of the Lord your God into the middle of the Jordan. Each of you is to take up a stone on his shoulder, according to the number of the tribes of the Israelites,*
*6 to serve as a sign among you. In the future, when your children ask you, 'What do these stones mean?'*
*7 tell them that the flow of the Jordan was cut off before the ark of the covenant of the Lord. When it crossed the Jordan, the waters of the Jordan were cut off. These stones are to be a memorial to the people of Israel forever."*
*8 So the Israelites did as Joshua commanded them. They took twelve stones from the middle of the Jordan, according to the number of the tribes of the Israelites, as the Lord had told Joshua; and they carried them over with them to their camp, where they put them down.*
*9 Joshua set up the twelve stones that had been in the middle of the Jordan at the spot where the priests who carried the Ark of the Covenant had stood. And they are there to this day.*

God made us to have memories. The nation Israel had several occasions that would help their country remember their journey. As the Israelites left their slave places in Egypt, they were commanded to begin with the Passover meal. The blood of the sacrificial lamb was to be sprinkled on the Jewish doorsteps so their firstborn son would be saved from slaughter.

Let me tell you a story I recently stumbled upon.

According to the U.S. Department of Treasury website, the motto "IN GOD WE TRUST" was placed on United States coins largely because of the increased religious sentiment during and especially after the Civil War, which divided the United States of America.

In fact, in 1864, the Union Army's motto, "In God We Trust," brought them victory.

When Secretary of the Treasury Salmon P. Chase was accepting suggestions about what to put in the new coins; he received many appeals from devout persons throughout the country urging that the United States recognize God on those U.S. Coins. It was a memorial to God, who had brought them through all their difficult years.

God instructed Joshua to erect those memorial stones to teach Israel to remember the past to claim their future.

This memorial (stones) is a reminder that; it's never their battle but the Lord's. The memorial stones representing each tribe of Israel were to instill their faith and trust in God alone. Are you able to keep a memorial?

Remembrance of God's goodness, breakthrough, favor, and mercy builds up strong trust and faith in the Lord almighty. Our failure to trust God stems from quickly forgetting the great things God does for us, especially in our past. Forgetfulness can prevent us from moving forward and achieving our dreams and goals due to the fear of the unknown; however, if you can trust God, who has brought you this far, you know He will surely keep you through.

The multiple memorials throughout the journey from Egypt to the promised land were made so that the people of Israel could teach their children about the great things God has done in the past and the great things that God is about to do in the future. The children seeing these stones will likely create a memorable image in their minds and be passed on to future generations.

When other people lose faith in God, it's mainly as a result of their inability to remember anything God has ever done for them.

If you can preserve monuments of God's goodness, it will remind you of how He pulled you through your past difficulties and enable you not to cease to wonder and be amazed at His greatness. Indeed, we need to erect those memorial stones in our lives.

Joshua chapter 4, verses 2 and 7 show that God wanted the Israelites to know that they belonged to Him (God).

*Joshua 4: 2*
*"2 Choose twelve men from among the people, one from each tribe,3 and tell them to take up twelve stones from the middle of the Jordan, from right where the priests are standing, and carry them over with you and put them down at the place where you stay tonight."*

*7 tell them that the flow of the Jordan was cut off before the ark of the covenant of the Lord. When it crossed the Jordan, the waters of the Jordan were cut off. These stones are to be a memorial to the people of Israel forever."*

It is interesting to note that Joshua instructed Israel to take up twelve stones from the middle of the Jordan River, where the priests were standing while Israel was crossing.

The middle of Jordan represents the deepest and innermost part of the River, where the water is most flooded, turbulent, and rigid.

These stones were gathered and transported from those raging waters and were delivered to a safe place. Each tribe had to carry one stone and put it to the place where they stayed in safety for the night. After they had gathered those stones, they became one family and children belonging to God. These stones were to become a reminder to all succeeding generations that they had utterly left Egypt behind. They have died to the old life of sin and are now delivered from that destructive and vicious life of sin and death.

This memorial was a reminder of their identification that they are now God's people.

In the same manner, when we come to know Christ as Lord and Savior, we must identify with Him. We no longer belong to ourselves but to Christ, who saved us.

That is why we have a memorial of our own; if you've been baptized, they understand that the water baptism symbolizes your personal and public identification with Christ.

The collection of stones reminds me of a vacation my wife

and I took in 2021 when we went to the Dominican Republic for the first time. During our vacation, we took a trip to an Island known as Saona Island. It is a really beautiful island, really organic and vintage, and its inhabitants are slightly cut off from civilization.

We had a great time. When we left the Island, I brought some stones, shells, and souvenirs. Any time I see these items, it reminds me of the beautiful times and great memories we had on that Island. Collecting the stones for me was intentional; I showed them to my children when we came back to the United States, and they were excited and couldn't wait to visit, too.

## MIRACLES OF REMEMBRANCE AND TESTIMONY

The Hebrew word for testimony comes from the root word Aydooth, which means to do it again. Did you know that whenever you remember something God has done in your life, you invite Him to do it again?

Revelation 19:10 builds upon that as it says "For the testimony of Jesus is the spirit of prophecy." When we testify of Jesus and what He has done for us we are remembering a previous deliverance which builds our faith to believe for a new deliverance.

This is why God instructs us to remember through His servant Moses and his prophets. God wants us to be continually filled with his spirit so we can continually experience more healing for ourselves and others, increased financial provision, and answered prayers. I want to encourage you to intentionally remember the things Jesus accomplished in the Bible so you can remind yourself He wants to continue to do those things in your life.

I also want to encourage you to intentionally remind yourself of the miracles God has done in your life. Remember how he came through and paid a bill you needed the money to pay? Remember how He healed you when the doctor said they could do nothing? Remember how He brought a great friend to you when you were isolated and lonely. Remembering these things will keep you full of God's spirit and faith as you declare God's promises over your life.

# 3 CHAPTER

# WHERE IS YOUR JOURNAL OF REMEMBRANCE

*"I will remember the deeds of the Lord; yes, I will remember your miracles of long ago. I will consider all of your works and meditate on all your mighty deeds." -Psalm 77:11*

One of the recurring themes that I've noticed in the Bible, especially the Old Testament, is the importance of remembrance. God calls His children to remember His goodness and faithfulness. The Psalmist made it clear in

Psalm 77:11 that he will consciously remember the deeds, miracles, and all the works of God's hands.

Since humans do forget, it is incumbent upon the called to remember all God has done.

In the book of Leviticus, God instructed certain weekly and yearly events of remembrance for the people of Israel. For example, the Sabbath was a weekly event to remember how God rested on the seventh day. The Passover was a yearly event to remember how God delivered the Israelites from Egypt.

The Israelites regularly created altars of remembrance to commemorate God's miraculous works throughout the Old Testament. For example, in Joshua 4, they stacked 12 stones to remember how God miraculously parted the Jordan River and let them cross on dry land.

David and the other writers of the Book of Psalms meditated on God's works and wonders. Their writings creatively remind the reader of God's past faithfulness and dwell on His goodness.
At the Last Supper, Jesus invited His followers to take the

bread and the cup to remember Him. We can testify that God calls His followers to be a people marked by remembrance.

Those who remember God's goodness are endowed with great power, while it is dangerous to forget His great deeds.

The Lord's goodness was forgotten by the Israelites multiple times. They will move through seasons of faithful remembrance and seasons of forgetfulness. Their forgetfulness sometimes led them into idolatry and oppression.

Let's look at

*Psalm 78: 10, 11, and 42*
*10 They did not keep God's covenant and refused to live by his law.*
*11 They forgot what he had done, the wonders he had shown them.*
*42 They did not remember his power the day he redeemed them from the oppressor,*

This story is typical of many believers; we are quick to forget all that God does for us. Forgetting all that God has done for us makes us very vulnerable to the devices of the evil one. We easily fall into his traps because we forget that all things are possible to God, and He has done it many times for us.

One becomes most exposed to anxiety when we focus our attention on our failures, disappointments, and pain instead of focusing on the many past victories from God.

When one focuses on all the wrongs in our life, the enemy attacks us with doubt, fear, and magnification of bad seasons instead of magnifying the God who is able more than able.

The opposite happens when we dwell on remembering God's goodness in our lives and always look back and recall our journey of blessings from God—recalling God's guidance, sustenance, providence, and all the different seasons of our lives. Most of all, remember His unconditional love and forgiveness of our sins.

The fact that I always remember the goodness of God in my life does not mean that I ignore any pain or disappointments in my life, but even in my moments of pain and hurt, I say to myself all things will work together for my good because God has done it for me in the past. I also ask God, please, I know there is something that you want to teach me through my season of pain.

As humans, it is always tricky in the beginning when we

go through storms, but it always works out to be good if we are willing to pay the price.

I want to share several practices that help me to dwell on God's goodness.

Daily Gratitude: Gratitude is the most potent weapon against anxiety, fear, and self-doubt. I do a daily inventory check of God's goodness and grace. These can include tiny moments like the grace to handle a difficult conversation, energy when I felt weak, or the beautiful, misty morning as I drove to work, finding parking on the busy streets of New York. Am always looking for God's handiwork in the small things gives me hope to see the bigger picture of His grace.

Reading old and new journals: I read back through my journals every year or so. Each time I reminisce about how God has been so faithful in my life, I am moved by the joy of the Lord, which gives me the strength to keep moving forward. I remember times when I felt lost and afraid, but God was at work in ways I couldn't see at the time. I traveled to the United States at twenty to begin a new life. I didn't know many people and had no parents but Christ and

Christ alone. I had to depend on God solely for everything.
On my journey to secure residency, 911 occurred which changed a lot of things in this country and created some level of fear, but remembering how far God has brought me kept me going. Sometimes, God will repeatedly use painful situations to draw us into deeper intimacy with Him.

David went through a similar situations when he was been chased by Saul.

Likewise, Joseph went from his dream to the fulfillment of the dream. God always knows how to bring us to an expected end. Reflecting on the many blessings of the Lord in my journals gives me a fresh viewpoint on current circumstances and renews my hope for the future.

As the Israelite people did in Joshua 4, while writing this chapter, I decided to pick some stones and begin to write about specific ways in which God has been faithful in my life. This creates a visual that is a powerful reminder of the way God's faithfulness builds upon itself in my life one day at a time.

One of the keys to surviving every storm is to remember the miracles and power of the captain.

Let's read about one of the storms that the disciples faced.

*Mark 6:45-50 (NIV)*
*45 Immediately, Jesus made his disciples get into the boat and go ahead of him to Bethsaida, and then he dismissed the crowd.*

*46 After leaving them, he went up to a mountainside to pray.*
*47 Later that night, the boat was in the middle of the lake, and he was alone on land.*
*48 He saw the disciples straining at the oars because the wind was against them. Shortly before dawn, he went out to them, walking on the lake. He was about to pass by them,*
*49 but when they saw him walking on the lake, they thought he was a ghost. They cried out,*
*50 because they all saw him and were terrified. Immediately he spoke to them and said, "Take courage! It is I. Don't be afraid."*

While on their way to Bethsaida, they faced a massive wind and were afraid. Jesus was not with them but knew what would happen to them and had already made provision for a way of escape for them. To touch on the power of remembrance, we will read in that same chapter a wonderful miracle that Jesus did. This was about a few hours before they faced the wind.

Verses

*34 When Jesus landed and saw a large crowd, he had compassion for them because they were like sheep without*

*a shepherd. So, he began teaching them many things.*
*35 By this time, it was late in the day, so his disciples came to him. "This is a remote place," they said, "and it's already very late.*
*36 Send the people away so that they can go to the surrounding countryside and villages and buy themselves something to eat."*
*37 But he answered, "You give them something to eat." They said to him, "That would take more than half a year's wages[e]! Are we to go and spend that much on bread and give it to them to eat?"*
*38 "How many loaves do you have?" he asked. "Go and see."*
*When they found out, they said, "Five—and two fish."*
*39 Then Jesus directed them to have all the people sit down in groups on the green grass.*
*40 So they sat down in groups of hundreds and fifties.*
*41 Taking the five loaves and the two fish and looking up to heaven, he gave thanks and broke the loaves. Then he gave them to his disciples to distribute to the people. He also divided the two fish among them all.*
*42 They all ate and were satisfied,*
*43 and the disciples picked up twelve basketfuls of broken pieces of bread and fish.*
*44 The number of the men who had eaten was five thousand.*

Jesus performed this miracle right before the disciples; Jesus dismissed the multitude and then informed the disciples to go to the other side. The storm came, and they had totally forgotten the power and authority they had. They had just witnessed a great miracle with many baskets full of food left.

The power of remembrance would have kept their faith firmly in the Lord, to know that Jesus would see them through.

**Let's now look at David**:
It will always keep you going if you can keep a diary of the many blessings, victories, and testimonies obtained through the mighty hands of the most high. That was one of the weapons David used when he faced Goliath. He remembered the strength the Lord gave him to defeat the bear and lion's attacks and knowing his God.

I keep a journal and read back through my journals. Each time I do that, I realize the many ways God has been so faithful in my life. I remember times when I felt lost and afraid, but God was actually at work in ways that I couldn't see at the time.

For those who know their God, they shall be strong and do exploits (Daniel 11:32.)

We are bound to face Goliath in our Christian journey, but it will take our faith in the Lord and remembering who He is.

Most of the Psalms that David wrote always depict his extreme remembrance of the goodness of the Lord, His mighty power, and realized that there is nothing he has received that God did not give to him.

David remembers all his victories, escapes, and his elevations. He ascribes all his successes to God.

*"I will remember the deeds of the Lord; yes I will remember your miracles of long ago. I will consider all of your works and meditate on all your mighty deeds." -Psalm 77:11(NIV)*

For he said, you come to me with a sword, spear, and javelin. But I come to you in the name of the Lord of hosts, the God of the armies of Israel. By calling the
I AM that I AM a name in the situation. God became what he called him: the commander of heaven's army. There was no way David would have lost the battle. We have the whole of heaven on our side; therefore, we cannot experience defeat.

*1 Peter 5:7*
*"Cast all your anxiety on him because he cares for you."*

In Philippians 4:6 the apostle Paul wrote, "Do not be anxious about anything, but in everything, by prayer and petition, with thanksgiving, present your requests to God."

***Now, let's look at-***

*Numbers 33:1-9*

*1 This is the route the Israelites followed as they marched*

*out of Egypt under the leadership of Moses and Aaron.*

*2 At the Lord's direction, Moses kept a written record of their progress. These are the stages of their march, identified by the different places where they stopped along the way.*
*3 They set out from the city of Rameses in early spring—on the fifteenth day of the first month —on the morning after*

*the first Passover celebration. The people of Israel left defiantly, in full view of all the Egyptians.*
*4 Meanwhile, the Egyptians were burying all their firstborn sons, whom the Lord had killed the night before. The Lord had defeated the gods of Egypt that night with great acts of judgment!*
*5 After leaving Rameses, the Israelites set up camp at Succoth.*
*6 Then they left Succoth and camped at Etham on the edge of the wilderness.*
*7 They left Etham and turned back toward Pi-haircloth, opposite Baal-siphon, and camped near Migdol.*
*8 They left Pi-haircloth and crossed the Red Sea into the wilderness beyond. Then they traveled for three days into the Etham wilderness and camped at Marah.*
*9 They left Marah and camped at Elim, where there were twelve springs of water and seventy palm trees."*

Life is a journey characterized by movements - detours, roller coasters, red stops, stop signs, and constructions on the way, which can create a delay.

No matter the delays, God will go before thee, and make the crooked places straight: I will break in pieces the gates of brass, and cut in sunder the bars of iron:" Isaiah□ 45:2□ □□□□□□□

In verse 2 of Numbers 33, God instructed Moses to keep a written record of their journey. There are many reasons why God wanted the Israelites to record the starting point of the journey and all the various stops they made. Keeping a record helps to measure your progress in life and to be able to develop faith and hope. Taking stock of where you are now enables you to show gratitude for the fact that you have not arrived yet, but you are not where you used to be.

The Israelites were not in the promised land yet; however, they were not in Ramsey (Egypt). The Israelites saw many signs and wonders in Egypt, including the 10 plaques. At one time, there was full darkness in all of Egypt, but in Goshen, where the Israelites lived, there was light. The angel of death came, but the firstborn sons of the Israelites were spared.

The remembrance of these signs should give everyone hope in the Lord.
God knew that mankind could forget His goodness easily, so He urged Moses to maintain a record of past events.

They came to the Red Sea on their journey to the Promised Land. For some people, the Red Sea is the end of their journey. Between you and your destiny stands the mighty Red Sea. Everyone will one day face the Red Sea.

They show up in marriages, businesses, churches, etc.
The massive Red Sea is in front of the Israelites, and the vast Egyptian army is behind them. Let's look at what the Israelites said to Moses. This is how human beings can easily be moved by a storm to change their minds and forget all the prior miracles they witnessed in Egypt.

*Exodus 14:10-12*
*10 And when Pharaoh drew near, the children of Israel lifted their eyes, and behold, the Egyptians marched after them. So they were very afraid, and the children of Israel cried out to the Lord.*
*11 Then they said to Moses, "Because there were no graves in Egypt, have you taken us away to die in the wilderness? Why have you so dealt with us, to bring us up out of Egypt?*
*12 Is this not the word that we told you in Egypt, saying, 'Let us alone that we may serve the Egyptians'?*

*For it would have been better for us to serve the Egyptians than that we should die in the wilderness."*
*13 And Moses said to the people, "Do not be afraid. Stand still and see the salvation[b] of the Lord, which He will accomplish for you Today. For the Egyptians whom you see Today, you shall see again no more forever.*
*14 The Lord will fight for you, and you shall hold[c] your peace."*

It was just a short journey, and the Israelites had forgotten about all the miracles and promises. These were the people who were in severe bondage, free, and on their way to the Promised Land.

They experience the first storm, and all of a sudden, they forget about everything and now wish they were back serving their masters. God will always make a way in the Red Sea if God sends you on a path; he factors the storms on your way. He goes before you and makes every crooked path straight. Never forget his goodness, as

you remember every testimony in your life; it will boost your faith and hope.

After the Red Sea experience, just three days later, they came to Mara, and guess what happened again.

Let's read-

*Exodus 15:22-25*

*22 So Moses brought Israel from the Red Sea; then they went out into the Wilderness of Shur.*

*And they went three days in the wilderness and found no water.*
*23 Now when they came to Marah, they could not drink the waters of Marah, for they were bitter. Therefore the name of it was Marah.*
*24 And the people complained against Moses, saying, "What shall we drink?"*
*25 So he cried out to the Lord, and the Lord showed him a tree. When he cast it into the waters, the waters were made sweet.*

In verse 24, the people complained against Moses. As you move on in life, you will come to a state of Marah (bitter situation).

Marah represents bitter times and difficult places in life, such as the breakup of a relationship, betrayal, loss of a loved one, backstabbing, and loss of a job. They were thirsty, found water, and were excited about it, but it wasn't very pleasant. Have you been in a situation where you find a glimpse of light at the end of the tunnel and get there to realize it was not a light?

Have you experienced shattered hope in your life? When you've prayed for the gift of the womb and gotten pregnant only to end up losing the baby. This is Marah. But God instructed Moses to pick a particular leaf, dip it in water, and it became sweet.

The Lord will always give you the refreshment you need on your journey; just remember his miraculous hands.

## THE POWER OF REMEMBRANCE IN THE COMMUNION

I want to remind you of a powerful tool given to us by Jesus, known as Holy Communion, The Lord's Supper, or The Love Feast. There is great power in communion.

Partaking of communion is one of the tools God has given us against sickness and disease. Not only sickness but any attack of the enemy. Communion aligns us with the body and blood of Jesus, and we also remember the fullness of what Jesus did at the cross.

Do you partake of communion often? In the privacy of your home? Pray about making communion a part of your life.

1 Corinthians 11:24 says; Do this in remembrance of Me.

The majority of people are familiar with communion, but they only experience it on special occasions or at church with their congregation. However, there is also power in private communion. The word communion (koinonia) itself means partnership, participation, and fellowship. It's an intimate act; it's a time when we become one with Jesus and what He did at the cross for us.

Why is communion significant?

On the last night, Jesus took bread and wine and He instituted a new ordinance for the church.

*"And as they were eating, Jesus took bread, blessed and broke it, and gave it to the*
*Disciples and says, 'Take, eat; this is my body.'*
*Then He took the cup, and gave thanks, and gave it to them, saying, 'Drink from it, all of you. For this is my blood of the new covenant, which is shed for many for the remission of sins."*
*Matthew 26:26-28 (NKJV)*

This was just before Jesus endured the cross, where His body was truly broken, and His blood was truly shed for our sins. For over 2000 years, the church has taken communion together to remember what Jesus has done for us on the cross.

***What are the elements of communion?***
***•The Bread:***

When we take it, we are reminded of the price paid for our sins and the healing of our bodies, Soul and spirit.

*"But He was wounded for our transgressions, He was bruised for our iniquities; the chastisement for our peace was upon Him, and by His stripes we are healed." Isaiah 53:5 (NKJV)*

• ***The Cup (juice/wine):***
Remembrance of Jesus' sacrifice on the cross and the New Covenant.

***Why does the church offer communion***

• A unifying sacrament where we remember our salvation

was bought by Jesus alone.

• It is the centerpiece of our Christian faith.

In Luke 22, we find Jesus greatly desired to eat this meal with His disciples before He went to the cross. Communion is all about the cross and what Jesus accomplished there. Communion is a mysterious fellowship, and many believers have had testimonies about it. Personally, communion has often broken the hold of the enemy in my life when it seemed nothing else was working, especially where healing is concerned.

A few years ago, I was feeling feverish with an elevated temperature, so I went to the Emergency Room. Upon multiple lab tests, I was informed of an elevated White Blood count but could not identify the cause of the elevation. Due to the levels of the complete blood counts, I was referred to a Hematologist. While waiting for my appointment date, I started taking communion daily for about three days.

On the 4th day, I went for my appointment, and the doctor ordered another lab. I waited for the results. When the doctor received the lab results, he was a bit upset about why they referred me to him because my lab work was 100% normal.

I had been healed by the communion and my faith.

1 Corinthians 10:16 says; the cup of blessing which we bless, is it not the communion of the blood of Christ? The bread that we break, is not the communion of the body of Christ.

When you eat the bread and drink the wine, you are becoming one with, fellowshipping with, and a partner with Christ's body.

When you do that, you become one with Him who bought back our right standing with God and all that He accomplished at the cross.

You become partners with prosperity, healing, wholeness, soundness of mind, and everything Jesus took back at the cross.

There is power in the communion, which does not lose its power. It brings you closer to Jesus. There is nothing else like it.

And remember, it is not only for healing but for everything Jesus accomplished at the cross and more.

## MIRACLES THAT WERE PERFORMED BY JESUS CHRIST

1 Jesus Turns Water into Wine at the Wedding in Cana John 2:1-11

2 Jesus Heals an Official's Son at Capernaum in Galilee John 4:43-54

3 Jesus Drives out an Evil Spirit from a Man in Capernaum Mark 1:21-27, Luke 4:31-36

4 Jesus Heals Peter's Mother-in-Law Sick with Fever Matt.8:14-15, Mark 1:29-31

5 Jesus Heals Many Sick and Oppressed at Evening Matt. 8:16-17, Mark 1:32-34

6 First Miraculous Catch of Fish on the Lake of Gennesaret Luke 5:1-11

7 Jesus Cleanses a Man with Leprosy Matt. 8:1-4,

8 Jesus Heals a Centurion's Paralyzed Servant in Capernaum Matt 8:5-13

9 Jesus Heals a Paralytic Who Was Let Down from the Roof Matt. 9:1-8

10 Jesus Heals a Man's Withered Hand on the Sabbath Matt. 12:9-14

11 Jesus Raises a Widow's Son from the Dead in Nain Luke 7:11-17

12 Jesus Calms a Storm on the Sea Matt. 8:23-27

13 Jesus Casts Demons into a Herd of Pigs Matt. 8:28-33

14 Jesus Heals a Woman in the Crowd with an Issue of Blood Matt. 9:20-22

15 Jesus Raises Jairus' Daughter Back to Life Matt. 9:18, 23-26

16 Jesus Heals Two Blind Men Matt. 9:27-31

17 Jesus Heals a Man Who Was Unable to Speak Matt. 9:32-34

18 Jesus Heals an Invalid at Bethesda John 5:1-15

19 Jesus Feeds 5,000 Plus Women and Children Matt. 14:13-21

20 Jesus Walks on Water Matt. 14:22-33

21 Jesus Heals Many Sick in Gennesaret as They Touch His Garment
Matt. 14:34-36

22 Jesus Heals a Gentile Woman's Demon-Possessed Daughter Matt. 15:21-28

23 Jesus Heals a Deaf and Dumb Man Mark 7:31-37

24 Jesus Feeds 4,000 Plus Women and Children Matt. 15:32-39

25 Jesus Heals a Blind Man at Bethsaida Mark 8:28-26

26 Jesus Heals a Man Born Blind by Spitting in His Eyes John 9:1-12

27 Jesus Heals a Boy With an Unclean Spirit Matt. 17:14-20

28 Miraculous Temple Tax in a Fish's Mouth Matt. 17:24-27

29 Jesus Heals a Blind, Mute Demoniac Matt. 12:22-23

30 Jesus Heals a Woman Who Had Been Crippled for 18 Years Luke 13:10-17

31 Jesus Heals a Man with Dropsy on the Sabbath Luke 14:1-6

32 Jesus Cleanses Ten Lepers on the Way to Jerusalem Luke 17:11-19

33 Jesus Raises Lazarus from the Dead in Bethany John 11:1-45

34 Jesus Restores Sight to Bartimaeus in Jericho Matt. 20:29-34

35 Jesus Withers the Fig Tree on the Road From Bethany Matt. 21:18-22,

Mark 11:12-14

36 Jesus Heals a Servant's Severed Ear While He Is Being Arrested Luke 22:50-51

37 The Second Miraculous Catch of Fish at the Sea of Tiberias John 21:4-11

# 4 CHAPTER

# THE PROBLEM OF FORGETFULNESS

Why is there so much emphasis on remembrance in the Bible? Forgetfulness is a common yet deadly spiritual disease. One of Moses' burdens was constantly warning the Israelites not to forget the Lord's deliverance and salvation. A similar emphasis is also seen in the New Testament.

The apostles saw it as part of their responsibility to remind the disciples of Christ of things that they already knew. Paul explained to the Roman church, "I have written more boldly to you on some points, as reminding you...."

(Romans 15:15). He sent Timothy to Corinth to "remind" them of his ways in Christ (1 Corinthians 4:17).

Peter declared his purpose in writing to his fellow believers: "For this reason, I will not be negligent to remind you always of these things, though you know and are established in the present truth. Yes, I think it is right, as long as I am in this tent, to stir you up by reminding you... (2 Peter 1:12-13).

One of the duties of a Pastor is to remind God's people of the Lord and His ways. Paul admonishes both Timothy and Titus to do just that (2 Timothy 2:14, Titus 3:1). He also encourages his young pastor friend to "remember Jesus Christ, risen from the dead, the offspring of David, as preached in my gospel" (2 Timothy 2:8). Forget this and Gospel ministry becomes impossible.

All of these reminders are indications that we tend to forget. Let's go back to the Lord's Supper. Jesus said, "Do this in remembrance of Me. Amazingly, we need to be reminded of the sacrificial death of our Savior. It seems unimaginable that, people who have been redeemed from the curse of the law, paid our debt which He did not owe, and granted eternal salvation would ever forget the One

who did all these for us. Well, humans forget.
Could this be a reason why we sin? Forgetting the magnitude of our sins and what it took Jesus to redeem us from them? Is this the cause of our complaints and murmurings at times? Remembering the salvation that we have received and knowing our redemptive package aids in us walking with authority, faith, and boldness. Forgetting easily is the reason why we get depressed, lose hope and joylessness, and walk in mediocrity. On the cross, Jesus traded our pain, shame, sickness, poverty, depression, and hopelessness for His abundant fulfillment in life.

Jesus Christ gave us the ordinance of the Lord's Supper to help us remember Him regularly. You can't partake in communion and still walk in forgetfulness. Forgetfulness is a great enemy of a joyful, faithful Christian life.

## PROSPERITY CAN CAUSE US TO FORGET GOD

Most people make mistakes with the money statements in the Bible. The Bible does not say that money itself is evil.

The Bible says that the 'love of money' is the root of all evil. Whatever you love more than God becomes an idol.

*1 Tim 6:10 NIV*
*For the love of money is the root of all kinds of evil. Some*

*people, eager for money, have wandered from the faith and pierced themselves with much grief.*

Consider these words of warning spoken by Moses to the children of Israel just before they entered into the Promised Land.

*Deuteronomy 8:12-14(NLT)*
*12 For when you have become full and prosperous and have built fine homes to live in,*
*13 and when your flocks and herds have become very large and your silver and gold have multiplied along with everything else, be careful!*
*14 Do not become proud at that time and forget the Lord your God, who rescued you from slavery in the land of Egypt.*

The Old Testament mentions a lot about the Promised Land, which is referred to as the land flowing with milk and honey. This figurative speech describes the abundance of God's goodness and the special provision that He has prepared for His people.

Do you know that God gave them cities and houses that they did not build, houses with harvest they did not produce, and water from wells they did not dig?

*Deuteronomy 6:10-11*
*10 When the Lord your God brings you into the land he swore to your fathers, to Abraham, Isaac, and Jacob, to give you—a land with large, flourishing cities you did not build,*
*11 houses filled with all kinds of good things you did not provide, wells you did not dig, and vineyards and olive groves you did not plant—then when you eat and are satisfied,*

***Moses warned the Israelites multiple times***:

"When you begin to enjoy all of this wealth, do not become proud and forget who it was who gave this wealth to you and who rescued you from your slavery…"

*Proverbs 10:22 KJV*
*The blessing of the LORD, it maketh rich, and he addeth no sorrow with it.*

It's very easy to be caught up in the pursuit of prosperity or the enjoyment of it and then easily forget the good Lord who got you there. Let's read this parable of Jesus about a man who became prosperous and thought he achieved all that wealth by his might.

*Luke 12:13-21*
*13 Someone in the Crowd said to him, "Teacher, tell my*
*brother to divide the inheritance with me."*
*14 Jesus replied, "Man, who appointed me a judge or an*
*arbiter between you?" 15 Then he said to them, "Watch*
*out! Be on your guard against all kinds of greed; life does*
*not consist in an abundance of possessions."*

*16 And he told them this parable: "The ground of a certain*

*rich man yielded an abundant harvest. 17 He thought to*
*himself, 'What shall I do? I have no place to store my*
*crops.'*

*18 "Then he said, 'This is what I'll do. I will tear down my*
*barns and build bigger ones, and there, I will store my*
*surplus grain. 19 And I'll say to myself, "You have plenty of*
*grain laid up for many years. Take life easy; eat, drink,*
*and be merry."'*

*20 "But God said to him, 'You fool! This very night your*
*life will be demanded from you. Then who will get what*
*you have prepared for yourself?'*
*21 "This is how it will be with whoever stores up things for*
*themselves but is not rich toward God."*

□According to this man, he has all he needs to be happy and self-sufficient; but listen to how the Lord responded to the man's arrogance. "You fool! This very night your life will be demanded from you. Then who will get what you have prepared for yourself?"

Money itself is not evil; It is not wrong to be successful.

What is wrong is when our success pulls us away from our dependence upon God. Paul wrote –

*1 Timothy 6:17 NLT*
*Teach those who are rich in this world not to be proud and not to trust in their money, which is so unreliable. Their trust should be in God, who richly gives us all we need for our enjoyment.*

Only God is completely reliable. I have come across many people in the church who are blessed financially and can support the church or are the highest tithe payers in the church. I have seen some who are very humble and see themselves privileged to be able to sow into the kingdom business.

I have also seen those who are very arrogant and will tell everyone they are the highest givers in the church, and without them, the church will collapse. It is the almighty God who takes care of His church.

There are also those rich people in the church who think that because they contribute a lot to the church, they should dictate what goes on in the church and even want the Pastor to bow to them.

It's easy for people to forget that a few years ago, they had nothing, and now God has blessed them to be a blessing.

Never forget the blessing of the Lord, which makes one rich and not our might. One important question we need to ask ourselves when we pray for riches or the blessings of God is the WHY. Why should God bless you? So you can brag or fulfill your selfish desires? Or so you can be a blessing to others and those in need.

## DO YOU LOOK FOR GOD WHEN ALL IS WELL

A Ghanaian proverb says, "Good times breed forgetfulness." Forgetfulness is one of the most common downfalls of humanity. God had some concerns when He delivered the Israelites out of the land of Egypt. He knew how easy it was for man to be faithful and true when he felt like he needed God, but He also knew how easy it was for mankind to forget about Him when hard times disappeared, too.

In Deuteronomy 6, we find Moses warning the Jews to always beware so that they don't forget the Lord who brought them out of bondage to the promised land.

Being forgetful has been a pattern for centuries and is still being repeated Today. I want to talk to you about the danger of forgetting God. History about the Israelites will prove that God's heart was broken most of the time and is still now when believers show ingratitude and keep sinning.

The Israelites, for a while, would be faithful when they experienced God's deliverance and got plenty to eat. Soon, they will drift away and forget about all the promises they had made to God.

Looking at the nature of men in the past, they are no different today. We tend to turn to God in times of need and then forget all about Him in times of plenty. We should always remember God—whether in the valley of shadows of death or on the hills of triumph.

*Ecclesiastes 12:1*

*"Remember now thy Creator in the days of thy youth, while the evil days come not, nor the years draw nigh when thou shalt say, I have no pleasure in them;"*

*Whether a man lives his life in success, prosperity, and ease or the pit of poverty, failure, and trial, we're all ultimately headed for the grave, where we must meet God face to face. What a tragedy if we've lived out our lives without remembering our Creator!*

***Listen to Solomon***:

*Ecclesiastes 11:9*

*"Rejoice, O young man, in thy youth; and let thy heart cheer thee in the days of thy youth, and walk in the ways of thine heart, and in the sight of thine eyes; but know thou, that for all these things God will bring thee into judgment."*

The world says, "Youth for pleasure, middle age for business, old age for religion." The Bible says, "Youth, middle age, and old age for your Creator." The Youthful seasons are seasons where we are determined to forget our Creator, but it's rather the season where we need to remember Him the most.

Let's remember that He made us, that He provides for us, that He cares for us, that He watches over us, that He controls us, and that He can save us, too. That's a lot to remember, but it's much easier to start memorizing when we are young!

## WHY REMEMBER YOUR CREATOR IN THE DAYS OF YOUR YOUTH

Why remember your Creator in the days of your youth-

1. **Energetic Years`**

We are most energetic during our Youthful years.

Why wait until our gas tank is almost empty before serving our Creator? Our Lord deserves our most vibrant and healthy years when we are very strong and enthusiastic about serving Him and working in the vineyard.

2. **Thoughtful Years**

Why do most of us accept Christ in our youthful days than in our middle age or old age?

I believe it's easier to receive Christ and repent when we are younger than when we are older. As we get older, our hearts are hardened, our conscience is seared, our sins are rooted deeper, and it is difficult to accept Christ.

3. **Teachable Years**

We learn more in our youth than in any other period of our life. I have come across a lot of believers who accepted Christ when they were older. Most of them have expressed huge regrets about how they wasted their life in their youthful days. They could have learned a lot more easily than they could now, and they could have invested more in the kingdom business than they could have in their older days. To those who led promiscuous lives and lost money, and those who have been infected with lifelong diseases, just to mention a few, as a result of the things they indulged in when they were younger.

4. **Dangerous Years**

The youthful years are years mixed with multiple ordeals: hormones, peer pressure, alcohol, drugs, pornography, immorality, testosterone, etc. Just a few people can steer through these seasons of their lives. Due to dangers that abound on every side, one is easily prone to temptations. Therefore, we need our Creator to carry us through this battlefield.

***Let me then help you remember your Creator***.

-Get to know your Creator: Study His Word using sermons, commentaries, and good books.

-Follow your Creator's order: He set and gave the pattern of six days of work followed by one day of rest for contemplation of His Works.

-Ask for your Creator's salvation: Even if your rejection of your Creator has broken you in pieces, He's willing to re-create you in His image.

-And while we're on the subject of salvation, I don't want elderly readers to be discouraged. You can always begin again. I have a question for you. Are you taking God out of your life or forgetting Him?

How do we forget God?

First, we forget God when we fail to thank Him for His blessings. We have all benefited from Jehovah God. Waking up this morning was the blessing of the Lord. Do you count your blessings? You might not be where you have anticipated to be, but you are also not where you used to be.

Everything in your life may not be like you planned it or hoped it would be, but sit down and start listing the blessings of your life and you'll be amazed at what an undertaking that is. Every bite of food we eat, the shelter over our heads, and the clothes on our backs are just a few of the multiplied blessings of God, especially in this land of abundance and plenty.

But how many times do people take their food and gobble it down without even bowing their heads in a brief moment of gratitude to the God who provided it?

*Romans 1:21(NIV)*
*"For although they knew God, they neither glorified him as God nor gave thanks to him, but their thinking became futile and their foolish hearts were darkened."*

It's a terrible sin when we forget God and think we can do everything by ourselves.

If you have a place to live, you need to thank God for that. If you have good health, thank God. If you have clothes to put on and a car to drive, thank God for that. When we are thankful to God, we remember our dependence on Him, and we walk more humbly before Him, which is what many of us desperately need to do Today.

Secondly, we forget the Lord when we make our plans without respect to Him.

*James 4:13-15*

*"[13] Now listen, you who say, "Today or tomorrow we will go to this or that city, spend a year there, carry on business and make money." [14] Why, you do not even know what will happen tomorrow. What is your life? You are a mist that appears for a little while and then vanishes. [15] Instead, you ought to say, "If it is the Lord's will, we will live and do this or that."*

You see, our lives and our futures depend on the will of God. When we audaciously boast of what we are going to do Today, tomorrow, and in the future, we should not forget the most important part of all our plans, which is the will of God, or if God permits. Why is this important? Because God holds our very life and breath in His hands.

He has our days and our years very carefully numbered. We don't know what the morrow will hold.
We don't know if there will even be a tomorrow for you or me, but we'll face God and answer for the lives we've lived here on the earth.

*Proverbs 3:5-6 NKJV*
*Trust in the LORD with all your heart, And lean not on your understanding; In all your ways acknowledge Him, And He shall direct your paths.*

Sometimes, we forget to consult God when we make plans for our day-to-day and future endeavors. We depend a lot on GPS, so why not rely on the Creator of the universe, the all-knowing God, the author and finisher of our faith? Begin to change the way you plan your life and future moving forward. Always keep God in everything you do.

*Matthew 6:33*
*"But seek ye first the kingdom of God, and his righteousness; and all these things shall be added unto you."*

It's very interesting to see the vows and promises we make to God in times of crisis and when we need a breakthrough from God. As soon as we receive our answers and in good times, we forget about all the promises we've made.

My dear reader, God takes vows that we take seriously. Have you ever, in desperation, begged God to heal you, a friend, or a family member and then made a promise to God that if He heals your loved one, you will serve Him, live a sinless life, go to church always, and read His word and as soon as God answers the prayers; the vows can't be remembered.

What I hear most in ministry is when believers pray for a job, their prayer goes something like this: "Lord, if you bless me with a job, I will not work Sunday but will come to church every Sunday and make sure I pay my tithe always." As soon as the job is secured, they are working overtime and having difficulty bringing their tithe to the Lord.

Unfortunately, our sinful nature tends to forget about God when the bank account is full, our kids are healthy, and our future looks bright. In those times, we often loosen our grip on God. We feel like we've got things under control. We can handle life. We become independent from God and dependent on our stuff.

I spoke to you in your prosperity, but you said: I will not listen (Jer. 22:21).

Prosperity has drawn a lot of people from the presence of God; this is mostly due to forgetfulness.

Prosperity causes the faithful to place God in the shadows, which increases our separation from Him.

True prosperity is not measured by income or in dollars and cents. True prosperity is becoming rich in God, being far wealthier by partaking of His divine grace, and worshiping Him in spirit and truth. This true prosperity is far greater and more important than anything else. Without faith and hope in God, we are living in spiritual poverty.

God warned the Israelites about this very thing. During those forty wilderness years, He met their needs day by day, and they learned to depend on Him. But as they stood at the edge of the Promised Land, ready to enter, God counseled them on the dangers of prosperity. He was about to lead them into a land abundant with water, food, and natural resources.

God knew that initially, they would bless and thank Him for His provision. But over time, as they got used to "having," their attitude would change. "But that is the time to be careful! Beware that in your plenty, you do not forget the Lord your God and disobey his commands, regulations, and decrees that I am giving you Today.

*Deuteronomy 8:12-15, 18*
*12 For when you have become full and prosperous and have built fine homes to live in,*
*13 and when your flocks and herds have become very large and your silver and gold have multiplied along with everything else, be careful!*
*14 Do not become proud at that time and forget the Lord your God, who rescued you from slavery in the land of Egypt...*
*15 He did all this so you would never say to yourself, 'I have achieved this wealth with my strength and energy.'*
*18 Remember the Lord your God. He is the one who gives you the power to be successful and fulfill the covenant he confirmed with your ancestors with an oath.*

We need to watch out for the good times! How often do we hear that? Probably not nearly enough. Prosperity and ease produce pride and independence from God. Because we live in a land of plenty, we must purposefully and constantly watch for this independent attitude.

I always tell my congregation that the battle begins after the victory. When you have received the answers to your prayers, that is the time for you to guard that which you have received.

# 5 CHAPTER

# THE WEAPON OF REMEMBRANCE FOR VICTORY

"The Power of Remembering"

The confidence David gained to overcome Goliath and the victory that was celebrated in Israel came from his remembrance of the strength and protection God gave to him. I want to conclude this book with these final spiritual thoughts and some scriptures that have helped me personally.

Putting remembrance into Action helps you overcome any storm or desperation and come out victorious.

What does this look like in practice? Psalm 77:1-20 gives an example-

*1 I cry out to God; yes, I shout. Oh, that God would listen to me!*
*2 When I was in deep trouble, I searched for the Lord. All night long, I prayed, with hands lifted toward heaven, but my soul was not comforted.*
*3 I think of God, and I moan, overwhelmed with longing for his help. Interlude*

*4 You don't let me sleep. I am too distressed even to pray!*
*5 I think of the good old days, long since ended,*
*6 when my nights were filled with joyful songs. I search my soul and ponder the difference now.*
*7 Has the Lord rejected me forever? Will he never again be kind to me?*
*8 Is his unfailing love gone forever? Have his promises permanently failed?*
*9 Has God forgotten to be gracious? Has he slammed the door on his compassion? Interlude*

*10 And I said, "This is my fate; the Most High has turned his hand against me."*
*11 But then I recall all you have done, O Lord; I remember your wonderful deeds of long ago.*
*12 They are constantly in my thoughts. I cannot stop thinking about your mighty works.*

*13 O God, your ways are holy. Is there any god as mighty as you?*

*14 You are the God of great wonders! You demonstrate your awesome power among the nations.*
*15 By your strong arm, you redeemed your people, the descendants of Jacob and Joseph. Interlude*

*16 When the Red Sea saw you, O God, its waters looked and trembled!*

*The sea quaked to its very depths.*

*17 The clouds poured down rain; the thunder rumbled in the sky. Your arrows of lightning flashed.*
*18 Your thunder roared from the whirlwind; the lightning lit up the world!*
*The earth trembled and shook.*
*19 Your road led through the sea, your pathway through the mighty waters—*
*a pathway no one knew was there!*
*20 You led your people along that road like a flock of sheep, with Moses and Aaron as their shepherds.*

The Psalmist starts in a place of hopelessness. Then he decides to 'remember the deeds of the Lord.' He meditates on God's miracles and mighty acts. This leads to an outpouring of praise and worship as he recalls the glory of God. No longer is he writing from a place of distance and despair and pain but a place of hope and remembrance.

By recalling what God has done for us and others, faith is restored, joy is uncovered, and our hearts turn from despair to praise. I can't stress this message enough.

I am where I am Today because of remembrance (Psalm 77:11-15).
One of my weapons to overcome the enemy and win battles is always to go for my journal of God's goodness and to read it.

As soon as I read and reminisce on the blessings of the Lord, my spirit is lifted and my faith is increased to deal

with the situation I am facing at that particular time. What it does is that the God who kept you through the other storm; will keep you through this storm too.

The following Psalm 78, written by the same author, encourages us to teach future generations about Jesus. We have the power to influence and inspire our children and their children by remembering what God has done.

I want to build a wall of answered prayers in our church, so that hope is made visible for the next generations. One million answered prayers will make up this landmark revealing a part of God's goodness. Making a record of testimonies will allow generations to remember Jesus' nature and His power to change lives.

Together we will inspire generations of God's goodness to turn their hearts from despair to praise.

Always remember good deeds and promises.

Let's look at David's faithfulness in remembrance-

*David and Mephibosheth*
*2 Samuel 9:1-8*

*1 David asked, "Is there anyone still left of the house of Saul to whom I can show kindness for Jonathan's sake?"*
*2 Now there was a servant of Saul's household named Ziba. They summoned him to appear before David, and the king said to him, "Are you Ziba?" "At your service," he replied.*
*3 The king asked, "Is there no one still alive from the house of Saul to whom I can show God's kindness?" Ziba answered the king, "There is still a son of Jonathan; he is lame in both feet."*
*4 "Where is he?" the king asked. Ziba answered, "He is at the house of Makir son of Ammiel in Lo Debar."*
*5 So King David had him brought from Lo Debar, from the house of Makir son of Ammiel.*
*6 When Mephibosheth son of Jonathan, the son of Saul, came to David, he bowed down to pay him honor. David said, "Mephibosheth!" "At your service," he replied.*
*7 "Don't be afraid," David said to him, "for I will surely show you kindness for the sake of your Father Jonathan. I will restore to you all the land that belonged to your grandfather Saul, and you will always eat at my table."*

*8 Mephibosheth bowed down and said, "What is your servant, that you should notice a dead dog like me?"*

David and Jonathan had a special bond; years after Jonathan died, David remembered the covenant they both had. He remembered the special love Jonathan showed him and the many times he provided a way of escape for him. David was indeed a good man. Some people forget easily.

In our ministry work, one will encounter many such betrayals and ingratitude. Pastors do a lot for their members, and armor bearers do a lot for their leaders, but most forget when they have reached a place of notoriety. May you always remember people who have been a blessing in your life.

Let's look at Joseph and the Butler-

*Genesis 40:9-14*
*9 So the chief cupbearer told Joseph his dream. He said to him, "In my dream, I saw a vine in front of me,*
*10 and on the vine were three branches. As soon as it budded, it blossomed, and its clusters ripened into grapes.*
*11 Pharaoh's cup was in my hand, and I took the grapes, squeezed them into Pharaoh's cup, and put the cup in his hand."*
*12 "This is what it means," Joseph said to him. "The three branches are three days.*
*13 Within three days Pharaoh will lift your head and restore you to your position, and you will put Pharaoh's cup in his hand, just as you used to do when you were his cupbearer.*

*14 But when all goes well with you, remember me and show me kindness; mention me to Pharaoh and get me out of this prison.*

*Genesis 41:9-13*

*9 Then the chief cupbearer said to Pharaoh, "Today I am reminded of my shortcomings.*
*10 Pharaoh was once angry with his servants, and he imprisoned me and the chief baker in the house of the captain of the guard.*
*11 Each of us had a dream the same night, and each dream had a meaning of its own.*
*12 Now a young Hebrew was there with us, a servant of the captain of the guard. We told him our dreams, and he interpreted them for us, giving each man the interpretation of his dream.*
*13 And things turned out exactly as he interpreted them to us: I was restored to my position, and the other man was impaled."*

Joseph interpreted the butler's dream, and the interpretation was extremely accurate. The butler was released as Joseph said it would be. He was restored to his assignment, and for over two years, the butler had forgotten all about Joseph until one day, through Pharoah's dream, he remembered Joseph.

What would have happened if Pharaoh hadn't had any dreams? Thank God he finally remembered.

I pray that we shall be remembered where and when we need to be remembered, and may we never forget the "Josephs" in our lives.

I just want to run through a few scriptures with you even as I conclude.

*Isaiah 49:15-16*
*"Can a woman forget her nursing child? And have no compassion on the son of her womb? Even these may forget, but I will not forget you. "Behold, I have inscribed*

*you on the palms of My hands; Your walls are continually before Me.*

*It is never possible for a nursing mother to forget the child who they are nursing, God said; even if that is possible, Jehovah God will never forget us. The Lord's eyes are always on his children. He is an example of the power of remembrance.*

*Deuteronomy 6:20-23*
*20 In the future, when your son asks you, "What is the meaning of the stipulations, decrees, and laws the Lord our God has commanded you?"*
*21 tells him: "We were slaves of Pharaoh in Egypt, but the Lord brought us out of Egypt with a mighty hand.*
*22 Before our eyes the Lord sent signs and wonders—great and terrible—on Egypt and Pharaoh and his whole household.*
*23 But he brought us out from there to bring us in and give us the land he promised on oath to our ancestors.*

Let us remember our deliverance, our blessings, and all the favors the Lord has showered on us, and let our children and people around us know so that they will know the power of our Lord.

*Psalm 103:1-2*
*1 Bless the Lord O my soul, And all that is within me, bless His holy name.*
*2 Bless the Lord, O my soul, and my soul forget not His benefits*

Man easily forgets- Our soul houses our will, emotions, reason, thoughts, and desires. The Psalmist was emphatic about the fact that he will make a conscious effort to make sure that; his soul does not forget the goodness of the Lord. We will be intentional.

*Deuteronomy 7:17-18*
*17 You may say to yourselves, "These nations are stronger than we are. How can we drive them out?"*
*18 But do not be afraid of them; remember well what the Lord your God did to Pharaoh and all Egypt.*

Have you ever experienced fear? I believe we've all experienced some type of fear once in our lives. One of the ways to deal with fear is when we can remember the times He delivered us from the cage of the enemy.

My dear reader, God bless you for reading through this far, and I believe this book has inspired you to always remember to remember. I remember when you started reading from Chapter 1, and now you are almost done.

My final thought is to always keep your remembrance journal; read through it all the time, and it will keep you through any storm. It will humble you and let you know where you started and how far the Lord has brought you.

This journal will make you praise and thank God always. May the Lord bless you, may He continue to remember His entire covenant with you. May your seed never lack and may the Lord be gracious unto you.

As you remember God daily, and make him the center of your life; you will always be victorious. Amen!

# THANK YOU

*I thank God for these people whose knowledge, support, and love directly or indirectly helped me immensely in writing this book. As this book is based on the power of remembrance, I want to use this page to remember the numerous people and those who will join me in the future. I might not be able to include every single person, if you reading this page; I want to say thank you.*

My parents Mr. & Mrs. Bediako, Mr. Kyei Mensah, Rebecca Aidoo, sibilings-Vatraut, Victoria, Helmut, Pastor Kofi Boye & family (London-VBC), Wofa Yaw osei, Andrew Morgan and the Morgan family, Yaw Gyasi, Emmanuel Barko Boafo, Pastor Nicholas Ankamah, Bishop Amo Brown, Apostle Ben Paul, My lovely big sister Lady Kirby Assuo, Apostle Ami Narh, MOBA 95, Pastor Azigiza & family, Kwasi Koomson, Steven Donkor and team, Winifred Ekuban, Rev. & Firstlady

Shalders, Denise Robinson, Edinam Cudjoe, Linda Liverpool, Pastor Kwame Acheampong, Pastor Steve Paintsil, Pastor George Aboagye, Pastor Steven Assifuah, Dr. Kofi Adjei, Dr. Gify Adjei, Ato Gyan, William Amenyo, Dr. Charles Konadu, Philip Arkorh, Presiding Elder Ormsby Asiedu, Samara Adjekum, Patrick Hayford, Abdul, Doris Abu, Gladys Abu, The Amankwah family, Amos Amarkwei, Pastor Richard Amponsah, Rev. Jahu Appiah, Elder Philip Arkoh, Elder Michael Ativie, Elder Nana Atuahene, Innis Baah, Bernard Bantum, Ato Gyan, Emmanuel Oteng Bediako, Quame Jr, George Boadu, Kobby Duah, Doreen Boateng, Sandra Ansong, Yaw Ansong, Joyce Mensah & family, Fritz Oakley, Micheal Nunoo, Yaw Atonsa, Ebenezer Doku, Eddie Hammond, Elgin & Mrs. Otoo, Emmanuel Ntim, Eseuoghene, Ev. John Sena, Pastor Eric Jeshrun, Evelyn Branford, Nana Koramah, Chris Gyamfi, Okyere Twumasi, Kingsley Manche, Elder & Mrs. Vincent Mensah, Jeffery Asiedu, Jerry Kansas, Nii Nortey, Dean Nathan, Dr. Kofi Adjei & Dr. Gifty Adjei, Jerry Laweh, Henry Amo, Mr & Mrs. Nyame, Noble Nketia, Van Vicker, Mr. & Mrs. Godfred Norman, Elder Sam Nyarko, Mr. Offin, Alison Owusu, Pedikuor Akufo, Dr. Charles Konadu-Adjei, Pastor Edmund Akplehe, Pastor G-love, Evangelist Samuel

Akufo(blessed memory), Patience Adjepong, Esther Aikins, Prophet Mc Olives, Lady Esther Quartey, Renee Wilson, Pastor Paul Boakye-Dattey, Ricky Asante, Paula Robert, Pastor Duwain Robinson, Evelyn Kwapong, Valeria Sosoo, Minister Bernie, Pastor Wallace, Elder William Amenyo, Ambrose Lawson, Deacon Kobina Ofori, Pastor Kwesi Nyarko, Pastor Joyce Ohene-Amoah, Mr. & Mrs. Isaac Abiden, Annette & Marcus Chanay, Willdrey, Fifi Folson, Lady V, Alexader Edwards, TD Jakes, Tudor Bismark, Bill Winston, Nii Ernie, Apostle Dominic Osei, Prophetess Lesley Osei, Prophet Nyan Boateng, Bishop Benjamin Manu, Mr. & Mrs. Amoh, Winifred Ekuban, Dr. Frimpong (Dada), Minister Emmanuel Ntim, Alston Osekre, Elsie Kwapong, Henry Kwapong, Minister Nana Osei (The worshipper), Rev. Samuel Opoku, Senior Minister Kofi Frimpong, Pastor Samuel Ampong, Apostle Ben Paul and Jr Ben Paul, Pastor & Lady Karen Mensah, Pastor & Lady Edward Amponsah, Apostle & Lady Awidi, Pastor Joe Beecham, Elder David Awuah, Dr. Wesley, Mayor Rich Rigoglioso (Mayor of Garfield), Pastor Harrison Sanchez, Apostolic church (NJ District), Apostolic USA Women's Ministry, Apostolic USA Men's Ministry, Pastor Steve Tetteh, Pastor Nii Abo Lomotey, Osei Tutu & family (Ohio), Michelle Adotey, Pastor & Lady Karen Mensah, Ato & Amy Gyan, Sarah

Washington, the Amoh family, Trevor West and family, the Afranie family, Agyin Family, Friend of College of New Rochelle, Friend of HSS, the Boafo family, friends of Panama School, The Ansong family, Jesse Morgan & family (RB Design Studio-cover design), the entire Apostolic Church World Wide, Dr. Doris Osei & family, Dr. Wesley, Odafe & family, Elder Ennim & family, Evangelist Ampaw, Willie & Mike, the Ayemedu family (Chris, Mimi, Nick), Deacon Tibua, Jose (Fair Lawn), the Abrah family, the Boakye family (1000 Morris), Joel Morgan, Ps. Ralph O'King, Rakka, Adjoa Bawuah, Gideon Asenso, Elder Out & family, The Krodua family, Gifty Mensah, LPBC-Ghana, Lorenzo, Pastor Listowel Mensah, Philip Asmah, Rev. Essel, Rev. Sammy Addy, Pastor Tim Godwin, Pastor Prince Donkor, Bro. Charles, Pastor Bright Abu, Apostle Samuel Appiah, Michael Kelvin, Kwamina Acheampong, Micheal Barketey, Stevoo, Henry Acquah Mensah, Vuga, Eric Mbimadong, Elder Jacob Mensah, Elder Vincent Mensah and family,

# REFERENCE PAGE

Davis RL, Zhong Y. The biology of forgetting—a perspective. Neuron. 2017;95(3):490-503. doi:10.1016/j.neuron.2017.05.039

Nørby S. Why forget? On the adaptive value of memory loss. Perspect Psychol Sci. 2015;10(5):551-78. doi: 10.1177/1745691615596787

https://www.verywellmind.com/explanations-for-forgetting-2795045
Article title Why People Forget by Kendra Cherry

https://www.treasury.gov/about/education/pages/in-god-we-trust.aspx

https://www.biblestudytools.com/bible-study/topical-studies/the-magnificent-truth-in-the-command-do-this-in-remembrance-of-me.html

https://www.learnreligions.com/miracles-of-jesus-700158

Brad Barton Exodus

# OTHER PUBLICATIONS

Connect with author: IG, FB, TWITTER, LINKEDIN, YOUTUBE

# THE AUTHOR

Nana Kweisi Bediako's first book was entitled What I Wish I Knew Before My 20th Birthday. In this book, he deals with the questions "If you could turn back time, what are some of the things that you would have liked to have achieved by now? What would you have done differently? What goals would you set?" His second book is "The Calm After The Storm".

Made in the USA
Middletown, DE
26 October 2024